Rejected
The Cancellation of the Qualified Worker

By Rebecca Benston

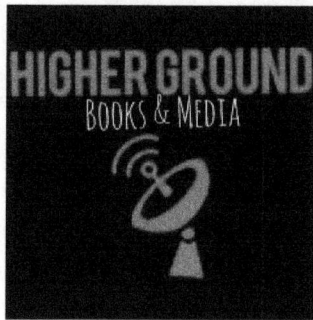

Higher Ground Books & Media

Springfield, Ohio.

http://highergroundbooksandmedia.com

Printed in the United States of America 2021

Rejected
The Cancellation of the Qualified Worker

By Rebecca Benston

Introduction

Have you noticed that it seems like people who hold management positions within most organizations never seem to know how to do the "management" part very effectively? Maybe that's too harsh. Let's try this. Have you noticed that in every organization, there are usually at least a handful of management-level individuals who don't seem to have the qualifications or the ability to manage anything? There is a reason for this; employers no longer seem to use the proper techniques to search for and acquire properly skilled employees for the positions that are available. They rely on either automated selection processes that lack the intuitive skills to select decent candidates or severely unskilled Human Resource managers and Recruiters who base all hiring decisions on popular opinion or trends rather than actual qualifications.

It's a bold statement, yes. But a true statement. And if you've spent any time searching for employment in today's job market, you have no doubt encountered this nonsense. And it doesn't really matter if you fall into one of the protected class categories such as minority, female, over 40, etc. Unless you know the secret handshake or the mysterious code words, you can just about count on being passed over for that job for which you were uniquely qualified. This book is about my experience as a 40-plus year-old, white, female who unfortunately lost her job after five years of service and consistently above-average performance ratings. I'm including a number of rejection letters in each section to give you an idea of what I've been seeing as I've patiently waited for employer after employer to reject me. There comes a time when we have to stop questioning our abilities and start questioning whether or not those who are in control are capable of making adult hiring decisions. At this point, I'm tired of leaving the fate of my career in the hands of those who can't be bothered to learn foundational skills but feel completely justified in throwing my resume in the trash. It's time to make some noise and recall the unqualified so that we can give the qualified a call.

Rebecca Benston

Chapter One – Who Am I to Say?

I spent about 8 years doing concentrated Human Resources work. During that time, I learned all about employment law, best recruiting and hiring practices, terminations, and staff development strategies. I conducted over 500 searches during this time for everything from Recovery Technicians for an Alcohol & Drug Treatment facility to Chief Executive Officers for chapters of a nationwide non-profit organization.

- I conducted numerous training events on topics ranging from sexual harassment to cultural sensitivity.
- I worked with others to create targeted workshops on topics such as secondary trauma for mental health providers, volunteer recruitment and recognition, and even a safety workshop that offered hands-on, interactive stations where participants could learn how to do things such as clean up hazardous, infectious materials and put out small fires.
- I conducted hundreds of interviews, created numerous search committees, and created a selection process that allowed for successful negotiation of hiring packages appropriate to the employer's budget and the candidate's skills/experience.
- I created a brand-new performance evaluation process that streamlined employee evaluations for a Joint Commission accredited organization.
- In addition, I counseled several employees and created performance improvement plans when necessary.
- I completely revamped our organization's salary scale to include incremental incentives based on years of service and level of education, as well as incentives to earn additional certifications.
- I was also responsible for handling any EEOC or Client complaints for one organization.
- I handled all calls for a four-state area for the complaint hotline.
- I was often the point of contact for complaints and for communications such as employee newsletters.
- There was also the supervision of three separate teams that were an integral part of our organization's successful delivery of service (reception/intake, performance improvement, and medical records). This amounted to supervision of about seven individuals.

All of this should be enough experience to at least garner an interview, however; these days it doesn't work that way. As opposed to the way I learned to do recruiting and selection (by actually reading and considering applications, scheduling preliminary interviews and calling back qualified candidates for a second round), today's selection process seems to go through an almost undetectable process. Dare I say, it is impossible for a hiring manager to get a good idea of someone's qualifications and skills when they've allowed a computerized sorting program to filter out any candidates who failed to use the correct buzz words. This is just one reason that I'm opposed to using Applicant Tracking Systems. They remove the responsibility from the hiring manager, and they severely limit any cognitively driven review of an applicant's qualifications. They also remove common sense, intuitive hiring, and a simple deductive reasoning process that is essential to making good hires.

I made so many great hires during my time as an HR Manager that it is hard for me to believe that the people who hold these recruiting positions can be content with allowing a computerized system to make these important decisions. Or worse, that people who have no skills or experience in recruiting or hiring would be entrusted with a process that so dramatically affects the business's bottom line.

I'm including my resume or rather, resumes in the back of this book to give you an idea of what I've been submitting to the jobs for which I've applied. This past year and a half has been extremely challenging as I've submitted over 1,000 resumes and received only five interviews (two of which were with a human being). I've applied for everything from a data entry clerk to a Human Resource Director. I've also been willing to take almost a $20,000 a year pay cut in order to just get a foot in the door.

I'm only 48 years old. I should be at the peak of my career; not starting over. However, politics (office and the other kind) pulled the rug out from under me when I had just celebrated my five-year anniversary at a job that was very much a part of my life. I was "eliminated" with little to no explanation. My evaluation scores had been consistently good, I was never behind on work, I had trained an individual to assist with my tasks and I was supposed to be trained to help with his. We shared the same title, yet the opportunity for me to learn his side of the job never seemed to materialize although I asked on several occasions. And when it came time for them to cut the position, I was sure that both of us were being hung out to dry. Turns out I was the only one left hanging. My younger co-worker was allowed to keep his job and I was told that there was no other position they could place me in although there were actually many positions available within the company. Make no mistake, it was personal. But personal is hard to prove. I tried. The Civil Rights Commission didn't see the problem with a 40-something woman with seniority being booted out and replaced by her 28-year-old male co-worker whose only real experience had been with this company. Nothing to see here.

At first, I was depressed. I felt as though I'd been slapped in the face and that all of the people I'd trusted had abandoned me. For the most part, they had. I had liked my boss and his boss. I'd had so many conversations with the two of them and we'd laughed and shared many stories together. We'd commiserated and strategized together. And I hadn't imagined that they would ever cut me loose so unceremoniously. Sadly, I'd been naïve to think that their friendship was genuine. I won't make that mistake again. I had just gotten my life rebuilt after a divorce and as soon as I'd started to feel that I had a handle on things, I found myself back at square one. But enough about that. The trauma has passed, and I am rebuilding my life once again. Though, at the time of this writing, the job search is still proving to be quite daunting, I am confident that I will find the right opportunity eventually.

In the time since my job was "eliminated," I've been taking every opportunity to learn new skills and apply them to my "side business" as a publisher. The business had been something I'd maintained with the salary I earned previously. Without a regular income, it is difficult to keep that business going. So, while I was waiting to be hired somewhere else, I invested my time and some of my money in completing the training to become a Social Media Pro. I watched countless videos on marketing and sales for publishers, I practiced my hand at creating attractive marketing tools and my business grew quickly, though it still hasn't reached complete self-sufficiency. The object was never to get rich as a publisher. I originally started this business as a ministry to help authors who were being rejected elsewhere or who were afraid to even try to publish. I wanted to help people tell their stories as it is extremely therapeutic to share our experiences with others.

When I lost my income source, my focus shifted toward building my marketing strategy and branching out into audio and video to promote our books. It's growing, albeit not enough to be my main source of income. Unless I somehow learn to live on about $150 per quarter, I still need a regular job to sustain myself and my daughter. After so many rejections, I decided maybe I should write a book about my experiences in the job market. I wasn't sure whether or not I should blame my lack of appeal on my age, my religion, my race, my sex or sexual preference, or just plain bad luck. Could be a combination of these things, but unless I talk about it, I may never be able to fully process it.

Being unemployed, especially these days, carries with it a great deal of shame. I've always worked for what I have and taken care of myself and my child. Only on a rare occasion have I taken help from anyone. I don't like to ask for help. I want to be able to do this myself. That's why I went to college. That's why I waited until I was 31 years old to have a child. That's why I have been willing to learn as much as possible about anything that I needed to know to keep my skill sets sharp. I can't just accept that no one out there wants a good worker who has good ideas and is capable of running things smoothly. So, I'm going to give you a glimpse into my inbox and show you what I've received over the past year and a half as I've set out to find a new career. I'm only sharing a small portion, but you'll get the picture.

In the back of this book, I'm going to share some tips and ideas for those who are searching for work and having the same issue. The job market is not as wide open as they would have you believe. No one who has gone to the expense of gaining an advanced degree should have to return to a life of flipping burgers or bagging groceries in order to make ends meet. This is not your failure. This is the failure of a system designed to cater to those who have learned what is unfortunately a much more sought-after skill than any of the ones I possess; the ability to kiss ass and blend in with a culture content to cancel you if you can't memorize pronouns that don't fit into the correct patterns of grammar that we've all been taught. It's time to bring back common sense and reliability. It's time for qualified workers to be recognized above those who simply know how to conform. It's time for us to get back to work!

Chapter Two - Human Resources...Imagine my surprise

I don't usually apply for HR positions with chain stores. Much of my experience has been in non-profit agencies, however, the skill set needed to be an effective HR Director is definitely a skill set that is adaptable to different industries. If you can learn HR for one industry, you can certainly learn the nuances of another industry when it comes to hiring, firing, and everything in between. Unfortunately, these companies don't seem to think so.

Update on ████ HR Director - East Area

Do Not Reply <petsmart+email+1m0f f89e17cfdc@talent.icims.com>   Mon, May 18, 2020, 1:14 PM

to Bb8372

Hi Rebecca ,

Thank you for your interest in a career with PetSmart. We've reviewed your profile for the HR Director - East Area role; at this time your background doesn't completely align with what we are looking for and we've decided to continue our search.

If you have applied to other roles, your resume will be reviewed for those roles as well.

Please continue to review ████ career opportunities at ████ and consider signing up for future job alerts via the "████" link at the bottom of the careers page.

Sincerely,
████ Talent Acquisition Team

This was in the original posting:

SUPERVISORY RESPONSIBLITIES

- Directly oversees 2+ Field HR Business Partners.
- Maintains a dotted-line relationship with regional recruiters.

EDUCATION and/or EXPERIENCE
Bachelor's degree from a four-year college or university and a minimum of 10+ years HR generalist leadership in business or multi-unit retail; or equivalent combination of education and experience. Knowledge of ████ employment law is preferred.

TECHNICAL SKILLS

- Must demonstrate business and financial acumen.
- Must possess excellent problem-solving, analytical and critical thinking skills.
- Must possess outstanding organizational skills, including attention to detail.
- Must demonstrate ability to build partnerships/relationships with internal and external partners, leveraging interpersonal skills to build trust.

- Must be able to multi-task in a fast paced, dynamic environment.
- Must be proficient in using the Microsoft Office Suite including experience with Excel, Word, PowerPoint, and Access.
- Must demonstrate a high level of intellectual, professional and interpersonal ability and flexibility.

To their credit, maybe it was a rather ambitious application. Not that I can't do the job, but I can admit that it is a larger territory than I've handled in the past. But we are supposed to aim higher, aren't we?

Your application to

Indeed <do-not-reply@indeed.com>   Thu, Jul 16, 2020, 12:07 AM

indeed

Application Update

Human Resources Generalist at ███████████████

Unfortunately, ████████████████ has decided not to move
forward with your Human Resources Generalist application at this time.

This was in the original posting:

Human Resources Generalist Requirements:

- Bachelor's degree required
- Specific knowledge of several human resources processes and practices (employment
  law/compliance, compensation, organizational development, leadership development,
  benefits, compensation, risk management)
- Ability to work in a fast-paced environment, superb organizational skills
- Excellent customer service skills and mentality

Still not sure why I wasn't granted even an initial interview. Although the job was in Chicago, I
clearly stated in my cover letter that I was willing to relocate for the right opportunity. So, with
such vague requirements, I should have at least been contacted to discuss my qualifications.

Still not sure why I wasn't granted even an initial interview. Although the job was in Chicago, I
clearly stated in my cover letter that I was willing to relocate for the right opportunity. So, with
such vague requirements, I should have at least been contacted to discuss my qualifications.

Your application to ████████

Indeed <do-not-reply@indeed.com>   Sat, Jul 18, 2020, 8:08 PM
to bb8372

indeed

Application Update

HR Generalist at ████████

Unfortunately, ████████ has decided not to move forward with your HR Generalist application at this time.

This was in the original posting:

Required Skills/Abilities:

- Excellent verbal and written communication skills.
- Excellent interpersonal, negotiation, and conflict resolution skills.
- Excellent organizational skills and attention to detail.
- Excellent time management skills with a proven ability to meet deadlines.
- Strong analytical and problem-solving skills.
- Ability to prioritize tasks and to delegate them when appropriate.
- Ability to act with integrity, professionalism, and confidentiality.
- Thorough knowledge of employment-related laws and regulations in California
- Processing and coordinating payroll on payroll platform
- Proficient with Microsoft Office Suite or related software.
- Proficiency with or the ability to quickly learn organizations HRIS and talent management systems.

Education and Experience:

- Bachelor's degree in Human Resources, Business Administration, or related field or equipment experience.
- At least one year of human resource management experience with payroll experience.

While I do have payroll experience, it isn't something I concentrated on as an HR Manager. But I could easily have picked it back up again. The problem is, I wasn't even given an interview where I could have discussed this with the hiring manager.

Application for Human Resource Manager at ██████████████

██████████████ <noreply@indeed.com> Unsubscribe
to Rebecca

Thu, Jul 23, 2020, 2:17 PM

Thank you for applying to the Human Resource Manager position at ██████████████.

Unfortunately, ██████████████ has moved to the next step in their hiring process, and your application was not selected at this time.

Qualifications

- Experience:
  - recruiting, 5 years (Preferred)
- Education:
  - Bachelor's (Preferred)
- Language:
  - English/Spanish (Required)
- Work authorization:
  - United States (Preferred)

Clearly, I had the qualifications. However, I didn't hear a peep from anyone regarding this position. I suspect this was one where I was over-qualified, but I'll never know.

Let's find your next opportunity!

The Mom Project <no-reply@themomproject.com>
to bb8372

Tue, Sep 15, 2020, 10:00 AM

APPLICATION UPDATE

Hi Rebecca,

We know this is probably not the news you were hoping to hear, but we promised to keep you updated. Your application for the HR Manager opportunity will unfortunately not be moving forward.

Jobs close for a number of reasons (some of which have nothing to do with the strength of a candidate's application), so please don't let this discourage you!

We are lucky to have an incredible community of talent here at The Mom Project (yes, that definitely includes you!), and we are constantly adding new family-friendly opportunities to match.

To help us keep looking for the best roles for you, please make sure to complete your profile if you haven't already.

One of many opportunities that didn't materialize.

Let's find your next opportunity!

The Mom Project <no-reply@themomproject.com>

Thu, Jan 7,
10:00 AM

to bb8372

APPLICATION UPDATE

Hi Rebecca,

We know this is probably not the news you were hoping to hear, but we promised to keep you updated. Your application for the Part-Time People Ops Generalist opportunity will unfortunately not be moving forward.

Jobs close for a number of reasons (some of which have nothing to do with the strength of a candidate's application), so please don't let this discourage you!

We are lucky to have an incredible community of talent here at The Mom Project (yes, that definitely includes you!), and we are constantly adding new family-friendly opportunities to match.

To help us keep looking for the best roles for you, please make sure to complete your profile if you haven't already.

I even tried part-time and contract positions.

Application for HR Manager at ████████

Hi Rebecca Benston,

Thanks for your interest in the HR Manager position at ████████. We are going to go in a different direction with the position. Thank you again for you time.

Sincerely,
████████

As you can see, the rejection responses I've received have included everything from a brief "no thank you" to a long-winded explanation as to why I'm not good enough for their company.

Chapter Three - Publishing/Writing…Not even this

Given the fact that I've been writing since around 2005, I decided that if I couldn't get back into a job that would allow me to use my HR experience, I would try to apply for some writing positions. At the very least, I had proof that I could write effectively. Or at least, I thought so. One would think that after writing a fiction series of ten books, several devotionals and empowerment resources, and even four children's books that my writing skills would be evident and possibly even sought-after by employers who were looking for writers. But this was also not the case. In my ignorance, I also submitted several applications for jobs in the publishing industry. Again, I found that just because I know how to do something doesn't necessarily mean anyone will actually let me do it. Some of these rejections really didn't surprise me, but they did make me a little angry. After all, the majority of these jobs were paying an average of $15,000 less per year than I'd made at my last job. So, even taking a pay cut wasn't a possibility.

Thank you for your interest in ~~Penguin Random House LLC~~

~~Peoplenet Notifications peoplenet@bertelsmann-hr.de via yahoo.com~~

Tue, Aug 18, 2020, 6:28 PM

to Rebecca

Dear Rebecca,

Thank you for your application and for your interest in the Editorial Assistant - ~~Penguin~~ position. Unfortunately, this position has been closed. It is our hope you continue to review our open positions online and apply to those that are of interest to you.

Thank you again for your interest in employment with ~~Penguin Random House LLC~~

Best,

Human Resources

~~Penguin Random House LLC~~

Application for Technical Editor/Writer at ████████ ████ ████████████

████████ ████   Tue, Dec 29, 2020, 1:05 PM
████████████ **<noreply@indeed.com>** Unsubscribe
to Rebecca

Thank you for applying to the Technical
Editor/Writer position at ████████ ████ ████████████.

Unfortunately, ████████ ████ ████████████ has moved
to the next step in their hiring process, and your application
was not selected at this time.

Thank you for your interest in Penguin Random House LLC

Peoplenet Notifications peoplenet@bertelsmann-hr.de via yahoo.com   Thu, Jan 14, 1:25 PM

to Rebecca

Dear Rebecca,

Thank you for your application and for your interest in the Publishing Assistant position. Unfortunately, this position has been closed. It is our hope you continue to review our open positions online and apply to those that are of interest to you.

Thank you again for your interest in employment with Penguin Random House LLC

Best,

Human Resources

Penguin Random House LLC

Let's find your next opportunity!

The Mom Project <no-reply@themomproject.com>

Wed, Jan 20,
10:00 AM

to bb8372

APPLICATION UPDATE

Hi Rebecca,

We know this is probably not the news you were hoping to hear, but we promised to keep you updated. Your application for the Senior Technical Writer opportunity will unfortunately not be moving forward.

Jobs close for a number of reasons (some of which have nothing to do with the strength of a candidate's application), so please don't let this discourage you!

We are lucky to have an incredible community of talent here at The Mom Project (yes, that definitely includes you!), and we are constantly adding new family-friendly opportunities to match.

To help us keep looking for the best roles for you, please make sure to complete your profile if you haven't already.

Thank you for your interest in

     Tue, Apr 13, 11:16 AM

to Rebecca

Dear Rebecca,

Thank you for your application and for your interest in the Managing Editor, Manga position. Unfortunately, this position has been closed. It is our hope you continue to review our open positions online and apply to those that are of interest to you.

Thank you again for your interest in employment with Penguin Random House LLC

Best,

Human Resources

Penguin Random House LLC

PEARSON APPLICATION | SMARTHINKING- WRITING TUTORS

Pearson Talent Acquisition <recruitment@invalidemail.com>

to bb8372

Thu, Oct 22, 2020, 2:30 PM

Hi There!

Hope you are well.

Thank you for your interest in the **Smarthinking Writing Tutor - Part Time (Work From Home)** position.

We especially appreciate the time and effort you put into the application process.

However, we regret to inform you that the position has already been filled. We will retain your information/kept on file for future reference, should an opening arise.

Feel free to let us know if you have any questions or concerns.

Best Regards,

Pearson People Services

Re: Editor (quality assurance) - Rebecca Benston applied on Indeed

███████████ @indeedemail.com>

to Rebecca

Dear Rebecca,

Thank you for applying for the Editor (quality assurance) position at
████████████

We carefully reviewed your application and have decided to move
forward with other candidates for the role.

We appreciate the time you invested to apply for this position at
████████████, and we encourage you to pursue future openings.

Best wishes for a successful job search. Thank you, again,
for your interest in our company.

-Human Resources

Your Application to

Tue, Mar 2, 5:40 PM
to Rebecca

Dear Rebecca,

Thank you for your interest in exploring career opportunities with Vista Higher Learning!

We've reviewed your application for the Development Editor (ELL) opportunity on our team and have decided not to move forward with your candidacy at this time. However, we will gladly hold on to your information should our needs change and we encourage you to apply for any future opportunities that spark your interest.

Thank you again for your time and interest. We wish you the very best of luck in your search.

The Talent Team at Vista Higher Learning

What really hurts about these is that I'm actually an editor and publisher who works with over fifty authors and has produced over 120 titles over the last several years. Though, as I've shared, my business isn't bringing in enough money to pay a salary. The authors who work with me and diligently promote their books, are paid royalties and some of them do pretty well each quarter. I do basic proofreading for each title I publish and I've even done freelance editing on occasion but am still not considered worthy of an interview for an editing position. I'm just not sure why none of this awesome experience translates into a recognized set of qualifications.

Chapter Four - A New Skill, Perhaps…Nope!

As I mentioned earlier, when I lost my last job, I decided to learn as much as possible about things that would help me to market my business. One of these things was social media management. I went as far as to pay for a course that resulted in certification. But it didn't seem to matter. I still wasn't getting a second glance as a candidate. What was it going to take?

Thank you for your interest in ██████████████████████

Peoplenet
Notifications peoplenet@bertelsmann-
hr.de via yahoo.com   Fri, Oct 16, 2020, 3:23 PM

to Rebecca

Dear Rebecca,

Thank you for your application and for your interest in the Senior Marketing Manager, Digital Content position. Unfortunately, this position has been closed. It is our hope you continue to review our open positions online and apply to those that are of interest to you.

Thank you again for your interest in employment with ████████████████████

Best,

Human Resources

████████████████████

Note, they don't say that I was not selected for the position. They say that the position was closed. The implication being that it was closed because someone else was selected. A roundabout way of rejecting an applicant, but okay.

Application for Social Media Community Manager at ███████ ██████████████

███████████████████
████████ ‹noreply@indeed.com› ████████
to Rebecca

Fri, Feb 26, 7:55 AM

Thank you for applying to the Social Media Community Manager position at ███████████████████

Unfortunately, ███████████████████ has moved to the next step in their hiring process, and your application was not selected at this time.

Blunt, to the point, not necessarily constructive. But thanks for letting me know.

Thank you for your interest in Penguin Random House LLC

Peoplenet Notifications peoplenet@bertelsmann-hr.de via yahoo.com

to Rebecca

Fri, Oct 16, 2020, 3:23 PM

Dear Rebecca,

Thank you for your application and for your interest in the Senior Marketing Manager, Digital Content position. Unfortunately, this position has been closed. It is our hope you continue to review our open positions online and apply to those that are of interest to you.

Thank you again for your interest in employment with Penguin Random House LLC.

Best,

Human Resources

Penguin Random House LLC

I've applied here several times, to no avail. But I do like that they continue to encourage me, even though none of these positions pay over $40,000 and they have no intention of considering me for any of them.

5/25/2021
Digital Communications Specialist
██

Job details
Salary
$40 - $50 an hour
Job Type
Full-time
Contract
Qualifications

- Bachelor's (Required)
- Project management: 5 years (Preferred)
- Events management: 1 year (Preferred)

Full Job Description
Seeking a Strategic Communications/ Engagement Consultant to work closely with other team members, business partners and leaders on a variety of strategic projects.
You will:
· Be involved with organizational engagement including internal communications (SharePoint posts and messages), supporting short video projects, and proactively addressing executives' needs.
· Assist in driving corporate events and meetings.
· Project manage deliverables, facilitate user sessions and coach teams to use new tools and techniques.
· Assist with Innovation and Culture initiatives, participate in project teams, and regularly interact with leaders across the organization.
Start: June 1st
Duration: 6 months
Location: 100% virtual/remote (Must be able to work traditional EST business hours)
Requirements:
· Bachelor's degree
· Excellent organizational and project management skills
· Experience leading virtual meetings and using appropriate tools (Teams, Zoom, Slido, SharePoint)
· 3-5 years of experience with a focus in organizational engagement, innovation management, and/or organizational culture
· Experience in a fast-paced, matrixed environment
· Experience with Microsoft Office, Teams and SharePoint
· Strong professional writing skills for a variety of audiences in a variety of media
· Video creation and editing experience is a nice to have (Vyond, Premiere Pro)
Keywords: strategy manager, project manager, talent management, internal engagement, communications manager, corporate communications, internal communications, employee engagement, strategic communications, program management, strategic initiatives, organizational engagement strategy, marketing strategy, content management, employee

communications, marketing and communications strategy, content manager, virtual producer, program manager, multimedia specialist, multimedia developer, instructional design,
Job Types: Full-time, Contract
Pay: $40.00 - $50.00 per hour
Benefits:

- 401(k)
- Dental insurance
- Health insurance
- Vision insurance

Schedule:

- Monday to Friday

Education:

- Bachelor's (Required)

Experience:

- Project management: 5 years (Preferred)
- internal communications: 5 years (Preferred)
- Microsoft Teams: 3 years (Preferred)
- Events management: 1 year (Preferred)

Work Location:

- Fully Remote

In less than four hours, I received this rejection letter.

█████

8:01 PM

Hi Rebecca Benston,

Thanks for your interest in the Digital Communications Specialist position at ████. After careful review of your credentials, it does not appear that you are the best fit for our needs. We will, however, keep you in mind for other opportunities that may arise.

Best of luck in your job search. Enjoy your day!

Sincerely,

█████

This one was particularly irksome in that I applied only three or four hours before getting this lovely rejection letter. To claim that they completed a "careful" review of my credentials is completely illogical and insulting. Maybe if they had at least waited 24 hours to respond, I'd have been inclined to believe that. But they were very eager to throw my resume in the garbage.

Chapter Five - Assorted Paths...since nothing else was working...

I even applied for jobs that weren't quite the right fit, but that I knew I could do if I started at entry level and learned as much as I could. I'm a fast learner and I'd always thought that any new skill was worth learning. The only skill I was learning at this point seemed to be how to take rejection like a champ.

Rebecca & ██████

██████ <no-reply@hire.lever.co>   Wed, Jul 1, 2020, 9:19 AM
to bb8372

Hello Rebecca,

Thank you for your interest in ██████. After carefully reviewing your profile, we've made the decision to not move forward at this time. We hope you don't mind if we reach out to you in the future when a position opens up that may be a good fit.

Thank you Rebecca
The ██████ Operations Team

Somehow, I think this one was an administrative assistant position. I haven't been an administrative assistant for over twenty years. That's the point of finishing your education and building on your past experience by learning new skills. But that doesn't mean I don't still know how to fulfill the duties of an admin. And if I'm willing to apply, it means I'm willing to do the job.

Update to your application

Indeed Hire <do-not-reply@indeed.com>   Fri, Jul 24, 2020,
                                                                 2:14 PM

to bb8372

Hi Rebecca,

Thank you for your interest in the Logistics Administrative Assistant - Work from
Home role at ███████████. We greatly appreciate your interest in this position, but
the team has filled the role at this time.

We hope that you will continue to use Indeed to find your next job as new opportunities
are added daily. Thank you again for your interest in this role and best of luck to you
with your search.

Kind Regards,
Indeed Hire on behalf of ████████████

Same as before. I wouldn't have bothered to apply if I weren't willing to do the work.

Your application to ████████████████

Indeed <do-not-reply@indeed.com>   Wed, Jul 29, 2020, 5:18 PM
to bb8372

indeed

Application Update

Author Representative at ██████████, Inc.

Unfortunately, ████████████████ has decided not to move forward
with your Author Representative application at this time.

Well, of course they have. Thanks for the extremely brief explanation. This really starts to feel like 9th grade gym class. We aren't picking you because, well, we just don't want to. Glad I'm getting to experience this all over again.

Job Application - Enrollment Coordinator- Chandler, AZ

Pearson Talent Acquisition <recruitment@invalidemail.com>
to bb8372

Tue, Aug 18, 2020, 2:38 PM

Hi Rebecca,

Thank you for your interest in ███████. We truly appreciate the time you have invested to complete your application. Please be assured that your profile has been carefully reviewed. We were fortunate to have a high number of strong profiles to consider for this role and unfortunately, on this occasion, have decided to move forward with other applicants.

We know emails like this can be discouraging, but we want to change that. While this particular position may not have been the right fit this time, we encourage you to keep exploring and we hope to be considering you for future opportunities.

Our CEO, ███████, states, *"We want ██████ to be one of the world's most efficient and best run companies. We want ██████ to be more digital, more service oriented, more customer driven, more agile, more innovative, more scalable in what we do, more able to share and learn, and more agile in the decisions we make."*

If the above statement excites you, we hope you will continue to explore ways we can do that together.

Please continue to visit our careers site ████████. Be sure to set up relevant job alerts so you will be notified when new roles open up. Stay connected with ██████ by following us on social media links below.

Here are a few thoughts as you continue your career search with us:

Applicants have greater success when their experience strongly matches our job requirements.

- Cover letters help us connect the dots between your experience and the job you want.
- If your experience is varied, we find that it can help to have several versions of your CV to match each job type.

We wish you the very best,
██████ **Talent Acquisition Team**

I feel so much better after this pep talk. Sadly, this makes about twenty rejections from this employer. And I believe I actually did get one interview from them. Not sure why I'm not a fit. Also, not sure why I keep applying, but they did say to keep trying.

Your application to Salience Learning

Salience Learning <recruiting+68554603@applytojob.com>   Thu, Aug 20, 2020, 2:01 PM
to Rebecca

Hello Rebecca,

Thanks for your interest in Salience Learning. Our hiring team has reviewed your application, and unfortunately, it was not selected for further consideration.

We appreciate the time you invested in applying for the position.

Again, thank you for your interest in our company and best wishes in all your future endeavors.

- The Salience Learning Team

In truth, I'm not even sure what this position was supposed to be. I have applied for so many. But the result, no matter what the desired qualifications, is always the same.

Thank you for your interest in ████████████ LLC

Dear Rebecca,

Thank you for your application and for your interest in the Design & Production Assistant - ████ ████████ position. Unfortunately, this position has been closed. It is our hope you continue to review our open positions online and apply to those that are of interest to you.

Thank you again for your interest in employment with ████████████████

Best,

Human Resources

████████████ LLC

At least they are consistent.

Your application for Learning Management System Administrator at ██████

no-reply@pinterest.com Unsubscribe   Sat, Dec 5, 2020, 1:25 PM
to bb8372

Hi Rebecca,

Thank you so much for your interest in ██████. We know that it takes time and energy to submit for a new role. Our recruiting team carefully reviewed your background and experience and, unfortunately, we won't be moving forward with your application at this time.

We do encourage you to keep an eye on our Careers page for roles that may be a better match in the future. Thank you again for taking the time to apply!

Sincerely,

██████ Recruiting Team

I've applied for several positions with ██████, but again, it's not in the cards.

Let's find your next opportunity!

The Mom Project <no-reply@themomproject.com>

to bb8372

Mon, Jan 25,
10:00 AM

APPLICATION UPDATE

Hi Rebecca,

We know this is probably not the news you were hoping to hear, but we promised to keep you updated. Your application for the Workday People Analytics Consultant (EST Hours) opportunity will unfortunately not be moving forward.

Jobs close for a number of reasons (some of which have nothing to do with the strength of a candidate's application), so please don't let this discourage you!

We are lucky to have an incredible community of talent here at The Mom Project (yes, that definitely includes you!), and we are constantly adding new family-friendly opportunities to match.

To help us keep looking for the best roles for you, please make sure to complete your profile if you haven't already.

Again, they are at least encouraging in their rejection. But an interview certainly would have gone a long way.

Regarding your ███████████████ online application.

███████████
██████ <springfieldcity+b16c5f91-
██████@applitrack.com>

to bb8372

Fri, Feb 5, 12:43 PM

Dear Rebecca Benston,

Thank you for your interest in the position of Printer #3371 with the ███████████ ████████████ Unfortunately, at this time your application has not been selected to move forward with this position. We appreciate your interest in this employment opportunity and wish you the very best in your pursuit of a position in keeping with your career goals.

Human Resources

Unfortunately, this one is personal. I have worked for this organization and I know from experience that they have basically blacklisted me. My former supervisor decided she had some sort of issue with me over a footer that I used to have on my e-mail. It had been absolutely fine while I worked in one building, but when I switched buildings, I also switched supervisors and this new one wasn't a fan of Bible verses. So, I was basically "canceled" as far as this place is concerned. I still apply in hopes that one day I will be able to work in the system again. There was nothing wrong with my performance. They just didn't like the fact that I was a Christian.

Thanks for your interest in Chainlink Labs, Rebecca

Chainlink Labs <no-reply@hire.lever.co>   Thu, Jan 7, 9:12 AM
to bb8372

Hi Rebecca,

Thank you for your application to Chainlink Labs! We're really grateful that you're interested in our work and would consider joining our team.

After reviewing your work experience, we've made the decision to not move forward at this time.

I hope you don't mind if we reach out to you in the future when a position opens up that may be a good fit - we are growing fast and we often get new roles added.

We appreciate your interest in Chainlink and wish you success in your job search. Hope to see you around in the community, and thanks again for your support of our work!

If you have any questions or want to continue the discussion, our Head of People, Ceri ceri@smartcontract.com is always happy to hear from you, so please don't hesitate to reach out.

Best,
Chainlink Labs Recruiting Team

This was basically an HR position, but I decided to add it here because it was a bit different. It was more of a generalist role, but again, evidently not the role for me.

Careers @ ██████████████   Sun, Mar 21, 12:00 PM
████████████████████████████
to bb8372

█████████████████████
Human Resources Department

Dear Rebecca Benston,

Thank you for your interest in the position of Communications Specialist with ████████████████!

Although you were not selected for this position, be sure to log in to your profile (see link below)
as you may have other applications you may be considered for at this time.

████████████████████████████

We wish you success and encourage you to continue in your academic and professional pursuits. We
also encourage you to remain informed of current employment opportunities with ████████████████
█████ by visiting our ██████████████████ webpage, and to apply for those positions for
which you feel qualified.

We appreciate your interest in employment with ██████████████████

Sincerely,

██████████████████ Recruitment Team

Since my plan is ultimately to move out to Arizona or Nevada, I did apply to several positions in
that area. No matter how many times you say that you are willing to relocate, hiring managers
don't seem to believe you.

So, this is another company I've applied to on several occasions. I don't apply just so that I can experience rejection. I am sincerely interested in working in this field on a more formal basis. As an independent publisher, I am able to do things my way and to learn at my own pace. But I would welcome the opportunity to work for an established publisher such as this one so that I could solidify my skills in the publishing arena. Again, I'm not sure how you break into this field. I evidently don't know the right people or grease the right wheels. Perhaps, that's the problem.

In any case, I think that this is an adequate representation of what I've experienced as a job seeker. I have hundreds of rejection letters, but the majority of employers don't even bother to send a simple confirmation. It is obvious that I wasn't considered for those positions, but it seems extremely rude for an employer to ask you to provide so much information to apply for a job and then not even take the time to look at what you've submitted. Ironically, it's just common courtesy to send a note to candidates who didn't make the cut. If I meet the minimum qualifications, I expect some acknowledgement. I don't pester the employer about the application because I believe that's rude, but I do expect that they will let me know if the position is no longer available.

I understand that hiring managers receive hundreds of applications and that it is difficult to review all of these in a timely fashion. I understand that logistics sometimes do not allow for a very personalized response. But any hiring manager should at least know how to create an automated response to send to candidates at all stages of the process.

Chapter Six - Is There Any Hope?

As rejection letter after rejection letter hit my inbox, I began to seriously question whether or not I was going to be okay. Thankfully, God had taken care of me through it all and I'd saved enough retirement money to support my daughter and myself. It wasn't much, but it paid for the necessities. No more vacations. No more fun. No more feeling accomplished. I'd have to stretch that money as far as I possibly could.

To add insult to injury, the pandemic hit, and companies decided to hold off on hiring until they had a better grasp on how their businesses would be impacted by COVID. Some positions I'd applied for were put on hold and some were simply eliminated. The majority of the companies I applied to didn't even bother sending me any notification that I wasn't being considered. Time passed and it simply became evident that it wasn't in the cards.

I decided to seek the assistance of a job coach. I'd gone as far as I could on my own and maybe my resume (even the one that I had purchased for over $100), just wasn't bringing results. I contacted a local office that works with displaced workers and began working with one of their coaches. She was very nice and tried to be helpful. I did everything she asked me to do, and we worked together to create a brand-new resume. I talked with her about the challenges I faced and what I was willing to do. She told me what she was able to do for me and we did as much together as we possibly could. After a couple of months' worth of sessions, it became clear that we'd exhausted all of our options. We parted ways and wished each other well. I was on my own again.

I've continued to apply for jobs. I took on freelance work to make ends meet. I did any kind of writing or critiquing or formatting that I could do. But clients were in short supply. Everyone was feeling the effects of the pandemic and no one wanted to spend money on freelance work. I kept putting ads out there and hoping for the best. Fortunately, I had one client who was able to keep me busy for a couple of months. But once we finished the work, I was back where I had started.

When I hit the 16-month mark, serious panic set in. If it hadn't been for those stimulus payments, I would have been in a world of hurt. They were just enough to keep my rent paid and some food on the table. But once every six months or so wasn't going to cut it. I didn't think giving people stimulus money was a great idea, given the state of our economy, but I couldn't turn it down. I needed it and although it seemed irresponsible, I had no choice but to be a willing recipient. The outlook for work looked more and more bleak. I had applied for every single job that I was physically and mentally able to do.

As a single mother, I also had to make sure that I had a job that would allow me to tend to my daughter's needs. I couldn't leave her overnight to take a third shift position. I couldn't really leave the house since she was doing her schooling online and sometimes needed help. My last job had been a Work-From-Home position and my life was built around that routine. I am not able to wear a mask all day due to asthma and I had never been strong enough to do manual labor. As I said before, once you've built your skill sets and finished your education, you should not have to go back to something you were doing as a teenager. Thirty years puts a lot of stress on a body, and I am just not cut out for certain types of work the way I was in my youth.

So, what's the solution? Do we just allow more experienced workers to languish while the compliant Social Justice Warriors take up all of the decent jobs? Or do we fight to get those positions back? At one point, it was necessary to try and level the playing field, but our efforts to minimize discrimination and bias have resulted in the inverse. Instead of giving minority populations a chance to be seen, they've made minority populations the only applicants who can be considered. Sadly, some companies have even gone so far as to try and push a truly discriminatory agenda on their employees through such things as teaching Critical Race Theory and attempting to force white employees to "denounce their whiteness." I can't think of anything more offensive than blatantly calling out members of one race and demanding that they be ashamed of who they are simply because of the color of their skin. It wasn't right when they did it to African-Americans and it isn't right as they are doing it to White people today.

Can't we just consider applicants based on their skills and experience? Can't the EEOC and the Civil Rights Commission simply do their jobs? Can't employers start to put the necessary time in to address the issue of hiring unqualified workers simply because they have a quota to meet? Or does asking the question automatically label me a racist? I sincerely hope it doesn't. Nothing could be farther from the truth! But if the social trends keep going in the direction that they have been, it's going to get harder and harder for some of us not to feel a little salty toward those who are being given opportunity after opportunity based on nothing other than the color of their skin. This is where the divisiveness comes into play. Any time a person or group of persons is given preferential treatment in the workforce due to characteristics such as sex, race, religion, sexual preference, etc., it leaves the door wide open for others to look at them as part of a growing problem. When I was a hiring manager, I looked at the education and job history above all else. And by education, I mean I looked at what they had studied and whether or not they had completed any programs rather than where they had attended school.

The only basis for giving someone a job should be their skills and education. That is all that should be considered. It shouldn't be that they were your sorority sister or that your cousin recommended them. It shouldn't be that they share the same political views as the hiring manager. It shouldn't be that the look a certain way, grew up in a certain area, went to a certain school, or even are a certain size. It should ALWAYS be based on their ability to perform the duties of the job. We've been doing this wrong for so long now, I fear that there are few out there who actually know what it means to make a good hire.

In Conclusion…Keeping the Faith

Although I still haven't found what I'm looking for (not a shout out to U2), I'm determined to keep applying for jobs until I find a hiring manager who will actually take the time to speak to me about my qualifications. Eventually, I have to find at least one. Someday, some desperate HR Manager will actually look at my resume and make the decision to call me. Someday, some small company that doesn't use an ATS will be thumbing through the resumes they've collected, and they'll see something on my resume that they like. And when my phone finally rings, I'll be ready to talk to them.

Until then, I'm still learning, still seeking, still praying that an opportunity presents itself. I'll freelance and sell everything I own if that's what I have to do. But I cannot believe or accept that there is nothing out there for me. I've got about twenty years left to rebuild my retirement account and I can't do that in bits and pieces. I need an employer and a new workplace to call home. As a young girl, I was waiting for my prince to come and rescue me. Funny how things change. Now, instead of looking for the white horse, I'm looking for a desk, a laptop, and a direct deposit slip. And if I'm lucky, some healthcare. But let's not get too crazy. I mean, human beings can't expect to be treated like…well, human beings.

Once upon a time, we were taught to be good, upstanding citizens who work and support ourselves and our families. I'm not sure when the story changed so drastically, but I'm not quite ready to forego my happily ever after. Recruiters, the ball is in your court. Somebody, pick up the damned phone.

My Resumes

#1

PROFESSIONAL SUMMARY

Innovative administrative professional with over 10 years' experience in coordinating and managing administrative programs. Strong flexibility in working as a member of a team, independently or in a leadership role. Consistently showing creativity while maintaining compliance regarding policies and procedures. Highly skilled in authoring business communications and compliance materials as well as other genres of writing. Experienced in utilizing all social media platforms as a marketing tool.

WORK EXPERIENCE

████████, Dayton OH
2014 to 2019
Policy and Records Compliance Coordinator
- Managed policy and procedure library containing over 1,300 policies via SharePoint.
- Developed and presented over 40 training sessions during 2018-19 regarding the creation of new or revised policies and procedures. Also delivered this training as needed for new employees.
- Created and distributed monthly Compliance newsletter for the Compliance Officer/VP.
- Collaborated with internal departments to ensure all policies/procedures are in accordance with federal, state and organizational regulations.
- Consistently conducted internal audits on records to promote accountability.

████████████ Springfield OH
2013 to 2013
Crisis Response Program Supervisor (Contract)
- Managed homelessness crisis prevention program by issuing rent vouchers to eligible families.
- Supervised HCRP Case Manager

███████████████, Yellow Springs OH
2011 to 2011
Executive Director (Contract)
- Provided leadership, learning opportunities for K-12 children.
- Developed marketing materials for educational programming.
- Wrote and submitted new and renewal grants for Creative Arts programming.

██████████, Springfield OH
2008 to 2011
Library Media Specialist
- Instructed K-6 students on how to search for and check out books.
- Streamlined supplies and materials by establishing relationships with new vendors.
- Coordinated Annual Scholastic Book Fairs for students and parents.
- Maintained inventory of over 3,000 books for K-6 students.

██████████, Springfield OH
2007 - 2008
Reference Associate (Part-time)
- Assisted customers researching information on various topics.
- Instructed patrons on accessing materials within the library or off-site.

Self Employed, Springfield OH
2006 - Present
Writer/Publisher
- Published author with over fifteen titles in circulation.
- Managed over 45 authors, illustrators, and narrators in the production of books, e-books, & audio-books through Higher Ground Books & Media
- Event Planning & Social Media Marketing
- Bookkeeping & miscellaneous administrative tasks

████████████████, Cincinnati OH
2004 - 2005
Human Resource/Volunteer Manager
- Managed the entire executive search process for 256 ████████ Chapters in the Great Lakes Service Area (Ohio, Michigan, Kentucky, and Indiana).
- Developed and delivered volunteer training for volunteers in the Service Area.
- Coordinated the Annual Service Area Award and Recognition Program.
- Handled all Complaints Investigations for the Service Area.

███████, Springfield OH
1998 - 2004
Administrative Services Director
- Managed all aspects of the HR department including, recruiting, hiring, onboarding, and performance management.
- Re-vamped salary scales to bring them in line with market resulting in wage increases across the board.
- Served as Staff Development and Safety Committee Chair; developed all mandatory employee training as well as opportunities for continuing education.
- Ensured credentials of licensed staff (nurses, recovery technicians, case managers, therapists, etc.) were kept up to date.
- Managed all client and employee complaint investigations for this JCAHO accredited organization.

EDUCATION
Master of Science, Human Services (Healthcare Administration)
Capella University
Master of Arts, Religion
Liberty University
Bachelor of Arts, Management and Human Development
Antioch University Midwest

PROFESSIONAL DEVELOPMENT/CERTIFICATIONS
Certification (Graduate) Pastoral Counseling

#2 (Actually paid good money for this one)

Qualifications for

HUMAN RESOURCES / ADMINISTRATIVE LEADERSHIP

HUMAN RESOURCES | ADMINISTRATIVE OPERATIONS | TRAINING / DEVELOPMENT | EMPLOYEE RELATIONS
EMPLOYEE ORIENTATIONS / ONBOARDING | MULTI-PROCESS OPTIMIZATION | BENEFITS ADMINISTRATION
DIVERSITY / INCLUSION | WRITING / EDITING | PUBLIC RELATIONS | WEB DEVELOPMENT | SOCIAL MEDIA
DISCIPLINARY ACTION | INTERNAL INVESTIGATIONS | BUDGET CONTROL | GRANT WRITING | EVENT PLANNING
MULTI-POLICY DEVELOPMENT | PROGRAM DEVELOPMENT | PROJECT MANAGEMENT | EEO / EMPLOYMENT LAW
MICROSOFT WORD | MICROSOFT EXCEL | MICROSOFT POWERPOINT | MICROSOFT PUBLISHER | SHAREPOINT

Highly Accomplished Leader who optimizes employee relations with a welcome open-door style by driving quality-focused recruiting, training, instruction, program, project, and policy / procedure initiatives, and who empowers a synergistic workforce to maximize an employer's success within highly competitive multi-industry sectors.

Influential Strategist who exhibits dynamic workforce design talents while maintaining up-to-date knowledge of industry trends to affect positive company change; who expertly aligns awareness of cultural, economic, and social matters to deliver results-centric policies; and who excels within highly challenging scenarios with strength and poise.

Engaging Communicator who recruits, hires, and onboards senior-level professional candidates; who develops solid relationships among executives, cross-functional teams, and the general public; and who leads peers by example and with ethics and integrity – always willing to "go the extra mile" to surpass a company's HR-based status quo.

Career Highlights Include:
- Continually driving strategic planning and accreditation readiness.
- Coordinating and managing staff development and compliance programs.
- Successfully writing and executing company-specific policies and procedures.
- Developing multiple corporate newsletters for compliance and organizational issues.
- Creating presentations on topics of personnel changes, safety, and sexual harassment.
- Developing comprehensive training and orientation materials for employees and volunteers.
- Concurrently managing 34 authors and 50+ projects to produce industry-wide marketable books.
- Achieving recognition as an Equal Employment Opportunity Officer and Client Rights Officer.
- Recruiting, interviewing, and hiring top-notch professionals with an emphasis on C-level searches.

PROFESSIONAL SYNOPSIS

HIGHER GROUND BOOKS & MEDIA
(2013 – PRESENT)

Editor | Publisher

Capitalize on the opportunity to lead forward-thinking review and approval of all author submissions for publication. Maximize publication success by driving results-generating sales, marketing, and event management for authors.

- Expertly perform innovative cover designs and dynamic formatting of all manuscripts.
- Promote authors via social media, including Facebook, Instagram, Twitter, and Pinterest.

██████████
(2014 – 2019)

Policy & Records Compliance Coordinator

Strategically steered coordination of comprehensive, compliant-driven review processes for 1,300+ policies and procedures. Coordinated quality analysis and key review of documents by committees and / or business owners.

- Coordinated learning and development programs.
- Communicated policy governance standards and processes.
- Managed a large-scale policy and procedure library for the organization.
- Led review meetings and electronic votes for annual reviews and off-cycle revisions.

████████████████████, SPRINGFIELD, OH
(1996 – 1998 | 2013)

Crisis Response Program Supervisor (2013) | Director of Client Services (1996 – 1998)

Delivered excellence in crisis response and client services, including administering HCRP program in Clark and Greene counties to align with network objectives. Approved rent assistance payments and applications for assistance.

- Skillfully managed a high-volume client caseload for a homeless shelter.
- Mentored families seeking beneficial housing, employment, and education.

██████████████, SPRINGFIELD, OH
(2008 – 2011)

Library Media Specialist

Proactively assisted public school students in locating materials from web and / or print sources by applying knowledge of wide-ranging authors, new releases, existing books in circulation, and library / technological resources.

- Instructed students on how to locate and check out materials.
- Cost-effectively managed supplies and materials ordering processes.
- Coordinated and managed high-attendance book fairs to boost the bottom line.

██████████████, CINCINNATI, OH
(2004 – 2005)

Human Resources | Volunteer Manager

Leveraged broad scope of human resources experience toward managing full-cycle executive recruiting initiatives for 256 chapter offices across 4 states. Conducted internal investigations. Administered benefits. Managed all volunteers.

- Coordinated and managed popular Service Area Awards and Recognition program.
- Led targeted onboarding, training / development, and performance management efforts.
- Recognized as the "go-to" resource for human resources and volunteer management issues.
- Rapidly investigated all Concern Connection Line calls directed to the Great Lakes Service Area.

██████████████., SPRINGFIELD, OH
(1998 – 2004)

Administrative Services Director

Played a vital role recruiting highly skilled staff, including physicians, nurses, recovery technicians, administrative staff, and case managers for this non-profit facility. Developed detailed job descriptions, policies, and procedures.

- Managed a Medical Records Department.
- Chaired an influential Staff Development committee.
- Successfully coordinated and led interactive instructional events.
- Executed Sexual Harassment, Crisis Intervention, Safety, and Infection Control training.
- Continually drove strategic planning and quality-centric performance improvement measures.

Additional Professional Experience

Writer SELF-EMPLOYED   2006 – PRESENT
Executive Director ███████████████████████, YELLOW SPRINGS, OH   2011
Reference Associate ██████████████████████, SPRINGFIELD, OH   2007 – 2008

EDUCATION, PROFESSIONAL DEVELOPMENT & TECHNICAL SUMMARY

Master of Arts in Religion (Emphasis in Discipleship Ministry)   LIBERTY UNIVERSITY
Master of Science in Human Services (Emphasis in Healthcare Administration)   CAPELLA UNIVERSITY
Bachelor of Arts in Management & Human Development (Dual Major)   ANTIOCH UNIVERSITY

Professional in Human Resources (PHR) (Formerly Certified) | Pastoral Counseling Graduate Certificate

Microsoft Office (Word, Excel, PowerPoint, Access, Outlook) | Microsoft Publisher | SharePoint | Social Media

Excellent Professional References Provided Upon Request

SUMMARY

Creative administrative professional with a solid background in Human Resources and Administrative Management and extensive project management experience from concept to development.

SKILLS

Microsoft Office	Employee Relations
Desktop Publishing	Supervision of Staff
Communications	Internal Investigations
SharePoint	Developing & Implementing Training

HRIS: Accurately administer and maintain/update HRIS employee database, processing new hire information, position/department changes, employee termination information, retirement and benefits information. Troubleshoot, resolve issues, explore advances/process improvements of HRIS database.

Benefits & Wellness: Provide support to employees on benefit matters, to include processing employee enrollments, changes and terminations, FMLA/Leave counseling, and auditing and reconciling benefit systems and invoices. Ensure ongoing compliance with federal and state regulations. Plans and facilitates annual Open Enrollment activities.

Recruiting: Sourcing, recruiting, and selection of new employees, including scheduling and managing interviews.

On-boarding: Onboard new employees. Conduct new hire orientations, including partnering with other personnel and service departments to provide the necessary resources to the employee.

Off-boarding: Counsel terminating employees regarding benefits and other questions; coordinate exit with other departments; process termination paperwork.

Documentation: Set-up and maintain personnel files according to compliance/legal standards.

Forms & Manuals: Prepare, verify, and/or review HR forms and reports for accuracy and compliance with established HR regulations, policies and procedures; assist in the updates and maintenance of policy manuals.

Process Improvement: Continually seek and implement process improvement-related ideas and feedback to enhance HR department efficiency, inter-departmental handoffs, and employee experience.

Vendor Management: Review and track contract agreements for execution by HR Director; manage day-to-day communication with vendors; implement, monitor, and troubleshoot vendor software upgrades.

Publishing: Review and approval of submissions; cover design, editing/proofreading, marketing & promotion of all authors, event planning; blogging, social media networking.

Policy & Records Compliance Coordinator
Dayton, OH
█████████ (Health Insurance)

Editor/Publisher
Springfield, OH
Higher Ground Books & Media

Library Media Specialist
Springfield, OH
████████████████████

VM/HR Officer
Cincinnati, OH
████████████████████Non-Profit)

Administrative Services Director
Springfield, OH
████████████ (Alcohol & Drug Treatment)

Child Care Worker
Springfield, OH
████████████████████

EDUCATION AND TRAINING
Master of Science: Human Services
Capella University
Minneapolis, MN, USA
Concentration in Health Care Administration

Bachelor of Arts: Management/Human Development
Antioch University Midwest
Yellow Springs, OH, United States
Dual Major

ACTIVITIES AND HONORS
Overcomers, Board Member
Public Schools Outreach for Christ, Board Member
SHRM, Past Member
Literacy Tutor, Warder Literacy Center

#4 (This one is the resume generated by Indeed.com)

Rebecca Benston

Experienced & Motivated Professional Ready to Jump Into a New Role!

I am an administrative professional with over 15 years of experience in coordinating and managing administrative programs. I am also an author who owns an independent publishing company that has worked with over 50 authors and produced over 120 titles since 2013. I am able to work as a member of a team, independently or in a leadership role. I consistently show creativity while maintaining compliance regarding policies and procedures. I am highly skilled in authoring business communications and compliance materials as well as other genres of writing. I am also experienced in utilizing all social media platforms as a marketing tool and I am highly skilled in all Microsoft Office programs including SharePoint, Publisher, Excel, and PowerPoint.
Willing to relocate to: Las Vegas, NV - Phoenix, AZ - Amarillo, TX
Authorized to work in the US for any employer

Work Experience

Policy and Records Compliance Coordinator (WFH)
█████████ - Dayton, OH
5 Years, 1 Month
DOCUMENT MANAGEMENT-Managed policy and procedure library containing over1,300 policies via SharePoint.
• TRAINING-Developed and presented over 40 training sessions during 2018-19 regarding the creation of new or revised policies and procedures. Also delivered this training as needed for new employees via WebEx.
• COMMUNICATIONS-Created and distributed monthly Compliance newsletter (using Microsoft Publisher) for the Compliance Officer/VP.
• PROJECT & TEAM MANAGEMENT-Collaborated with internal departments to ensure all policies/procedures are in accordance with federal, state and organizational regulations.
• AUDITING-Consistently conducted internal audits on records to promote accountability.

Human Resource/Volunteer Manager
█████████████ - Cincinnati, OH
1 Year, 4 Months
RECRUITING/TALENT ACQUISITION-Managed the entire executive search process for256 ████████ Chapters in the Great Lakes Service Area (Ohio, Michigan, Kentucky, and Indiana).
• TRAINING-Developed and delivered volunteer training for volunteers in the Service Area.
• VOLUNTEER ADMINISTRATION-Coordinated the Annual Service Area Award and Recognition Program.
• INTERNAL INVESTIGATIONS-Handled all Complaints Investigations for the Service Area.

Administrative Services Director
█████████ - Springfield, OH
6 Years, 2 Months
HUMAN RESOURCES-Managed all aspects of the HR department including, recruiting, hiring, onboarding, and performance management.
• WAGE ADMINISTRATION-Re-vamped salary scales to bring them in line with market resulting in wage increases across the board.
• COMMITTEE CHAIR-Served as Staff Development and Safety Committee Chair; developed all mandatory employee training as well as opportunities for continuing education.
• CREDENTIALING-Ensured credentials of licensed staff (nurses, recovery technicians, case managers, therapists, etc.) were kept up to date.
• REGULATORY/INTERNAL INVESTIGATIONS-Managed all client and employee complaint investigations for this JCAHO accredited organization.

Client Services Director (Regular)/Crisis Response Program Supervisor (Contract)

- Springfield, OH

1 Year

Springfield OH1996 to 1998 and 2013Client Services Director (Regular)/Crisis Response Program Supervisor (Contract)
• PROGRAM MANAGEMENT-Managed homelessness crisis prevention program by issuing rent vouchers to eligible families.
• STAFF SUPERVISION-Supervised HCRP Case Manager

Education

Master of Science in Human Services
Capella University

Bachelor of Arts in Management and Human Development
Antioch University Midwest

Resources

Resume Writing

HGBM Services offers assistance with resume writing. HGBM can use an old resume or even a list of experience and education to create a professional resume for you. Reasonable rates. Quick turnaround. Contact them at highergroundbooksandmedia@gmail.com for more information.

Job Boards

Here is a list of job boards used by the author in her job search:

Indeed.com

The Mom Project – www.themomproject.com

Craigslist – www.craigslist.com

Ohio Means Jobs - https://omj.ohio.gov/

LinkedIn Jobs – www.linkedin.com

Zip Recruiting – www.ziprecruiter.com

Rat Race Rebellion – https://ratracerebellion.com/

And many more, including contacting specific companies directly.

Career Aptitude

Here are some resources for determining what types of jobs are the best fit for you:

Indeed.com - https://www.indeed.com/career-advice/finding-a-job/free-career-aptitude-tests-for-adults

The Balance Careers - https://www.thebalancecareers.com/free-career-aptitude-tests-2059813

Call for Submissions

Higher Ground Books & Media/Bulletproof Books is accepting your stories for an anthology about wrongful termination and workplace discrimination called Dismissed! If you're interested in adding our story to this collection, please send your submission to us at highergroundbooksandmedia@gmail.com by October 31, 2021.

MARY USED TO HAVE A JOB...

MARY USED TO HAVE A JOB
HAVE A JOB
HAVE A JOB
MARY USED TO HAVE A JOB
THAT HELPED HER PAY HER BILLS.

THEN ONE DAY THEY MADE HER TRAIN
MADE HER TRAIN
MADE HER TRAIN
THEN ONE DAY THEY MADE HER TRAIN
A YOUNGER MAN NAMED JIM.

WHEN SHE FINISHED TRAINING JIM
TRAINING JIM
TRAINING JIM
WHEN SHE FINISHED TRAINING JIM,
THEY GAVE HER JOB TO HIM.

Has this ever happened to you? It's time to tell your story. Message me for more information. All participants will be kept confidential. It's time to speak up. Let's tell your story!

Other titles from Higher Ground Books & Media:

Don't Be Stupid (And I Mean That in the Nicest Way) by Rebecca Benston

Single, Sober, & Serious by Rebecca Benston

Wise Up to Rise Up by Rebecca Benston

Forgiven and Not Forgotten by Terra Kern

Domestic by H.S. Daniels

Miracles: I Love Them by Forest Godin

Slumberland by Derra Nicole Sabo

Through the Sliver of a Frosted Window by Robin Lynn Melet

Raven Transcending Fear by Terri Kozlowski

Out of Darkness by Stephen Bowman

Redeeming Gethsemane by Daniel K. Held

Eyes of Understanding by Stephen Shepherd

My Name is Sam…And Heaven is Still Shining Through by Joe Siccardi

Add these titles to your collection today!

http://www.highergroundbooksandmedia.com

Do you have a story to tell?

Higher Ground Books & Media is an independent Christian-based publisher specializing in stories of triumph! Our purpose is to empower, inspire, and educate through the sharing of personal experiences.

Please visit our website for our submission guidelines.

http://www.highergroundbooksandmedia.com

www.ingramcontent.com/pod-product-compliance
Lightning Source LLC
Chambersburg PA
CBHW051233200326
41519CB00025B/7357